The Age of Dinosaurs

Meet Tyrannosaurus Rex

Written by Jayne Raymond

Illustrations by Leonello Calvetti and Luca Massini

 Cavendish Square

New York

Published in 2014 by Cavendish Square Publishing, LLC
303 Park Avenue South, Suite 1247, New York, NY 10010

Library of Congress Cataloging-in-Publication Data

Raymond, Jayne.
Meet tyrannosaurus rex / by Jayne Raymond.
p. cm. — (The age of dinosaurs)
Includes index.
ISBN 978-1-62712-598-7 (hardcover) ISBN 978-1-62712-599-4 (paperback) ISBN 978-1-62712-600-7 (ebook)
1. Tyrannosaurus rex — Juvenile literature. I. Raymond, Jayne. II. Title.
QE862.S3 D35 2014
567.912—dc23

Editorial Director: Dean Miller
Art Director: Jeffrey Talbot
Designer: Joseph Macri
Photo Researcher: Julie Alissi, J8 Media
Production Editor: Andrew Coddington

Illustrations by Leonello Calvetti and Luca Massini.

The photographs used in this book and by permission and through the courtesy of: Lynn Koenig/Flickr/Getty Images, 8; Debi Bishop/Vetta/Getty Images, 8; Ben Klaus/Vetta/Getty Images, 8; House Light Gallery - Steven House Photography/Flickr/Getty Images, 8; Harold William Menke/ DiplodocusWyoming/ http://research.amnh.org/paleontology/photographs/1897-wyoming-jurassic/00.html, 20; Christophe Hendrickx/Tyrannosaurus 4040, 21; AP Photo/Emile Wamsteker, 21.

Printed in the United States of America

CONTENTS

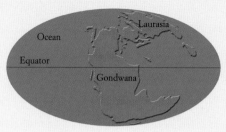

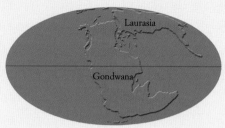

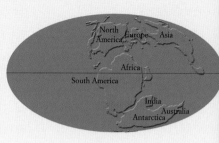

| Late Triassic | Early Jurassic | Middle Jurassic |
| 227 – 206 million years ago. | 206 – 176 million years ago. | 176 – 159 million years ago. |

A CHANGING WORLD

Earth's long history began 4.6 billion years ago. Dinosaurs were among the most fascinating animals from Earth's long past.

The word "dinosaur" originates from the Greek words *deinos* and *sauros*, which together mean "fearfully great lizards."

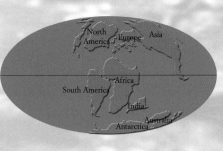
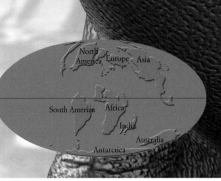

Late Jurassic	Early Cretaceous	Late Cretaceous
159 – 144 million years ago.	144 – 99 million years ago.	99 – 65 million years ago.

To understand dinosaurs we need to understand geological time, the lifetime of our planet. Earth history is divided into eras, periods, epochs, and ages. The dinosaur era, called the Mesozoic Era, is divided in three periods: Triassic, which lasted 42 million years; Jurassic, 61 million years; and Cretaceous, 79 million years. Dinosaurs ruled the world for over 160 million years.

Man never met dinosaurs. They had disappeared nearly 65 million years before man's appearance on Earth.

The dinosaur world differed from our world. The climate was warmer, the continents were different, and grass did not even exist!

A HUNGRY GIANT

An adult Tyrannosaurus Rex (often shortened to T-Rex) could grow to 42 feet long and 13 feet high, and it could weigh more than 7 tons. The T-Rex's enormous head was about 5 feet long, and its jaws contained 58 large teeth which were serrated and pointed. These teeth were 3-6 inches long and about 1 inch wide. Surely the sight of an attacking T-Rex would have been terrifying!

However, despite its body size, the T-Rex's brain was no larger than 11 inches. From the shape of its brain, we know that T-Rex had a well-developed sense of smell, for identifying distant sources of food.

FINDING TYRANNOSAURUS REX

Sixty-five million years ago, T-Rex lived in coastal plains bordering a shallow sea which extended from the Gulf of Mexico to the Arctic Ocean and divided present-day North America into two parts. Skeletal remains of T-Rex have been discovered in Alberta, Saskatchewan, Montana, North Dakota, South Dakota, Wyoming, Colorado, Texas, and Mexico.

Alberta, Canada

Montana

Colorado

Chihuahua, Mexico

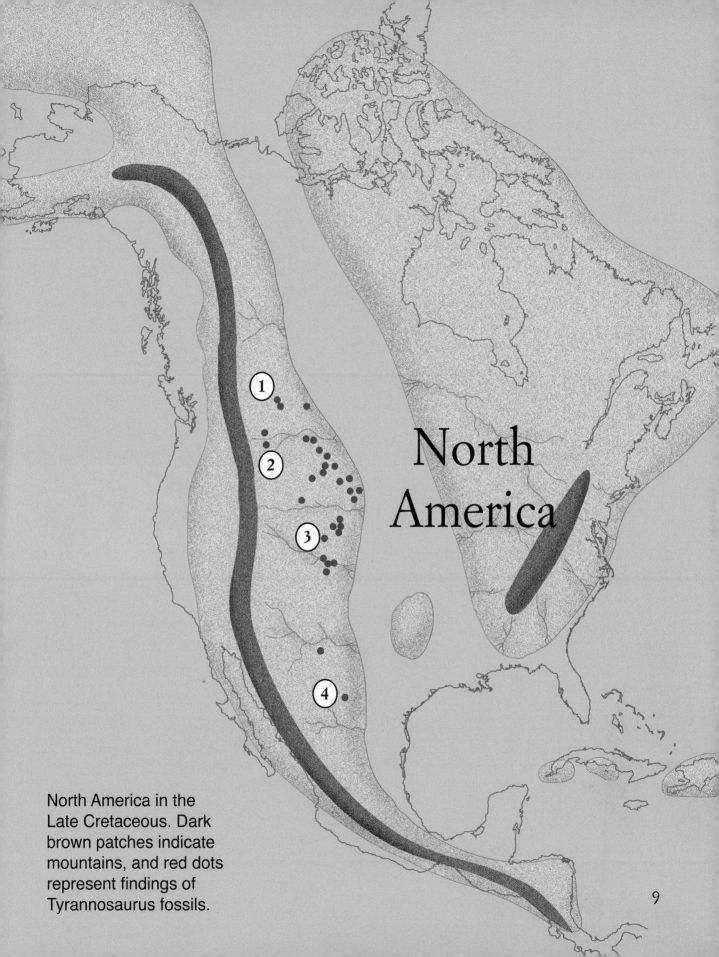

North America in the Late Cretaceous. Dark brown patches indicate mountains, and red dots represent findings of Tyrannosaurus fossils.

North America

9

BIRTH

T-Rex babies were hatched from large eggs with wrinkled shells. The mother dug a nest in the mud where she would lay her eggs. The parents kept watch over the nest, much like present-day crocodiles, to make sure that eggs and hatchlings did not fall victim to predators.

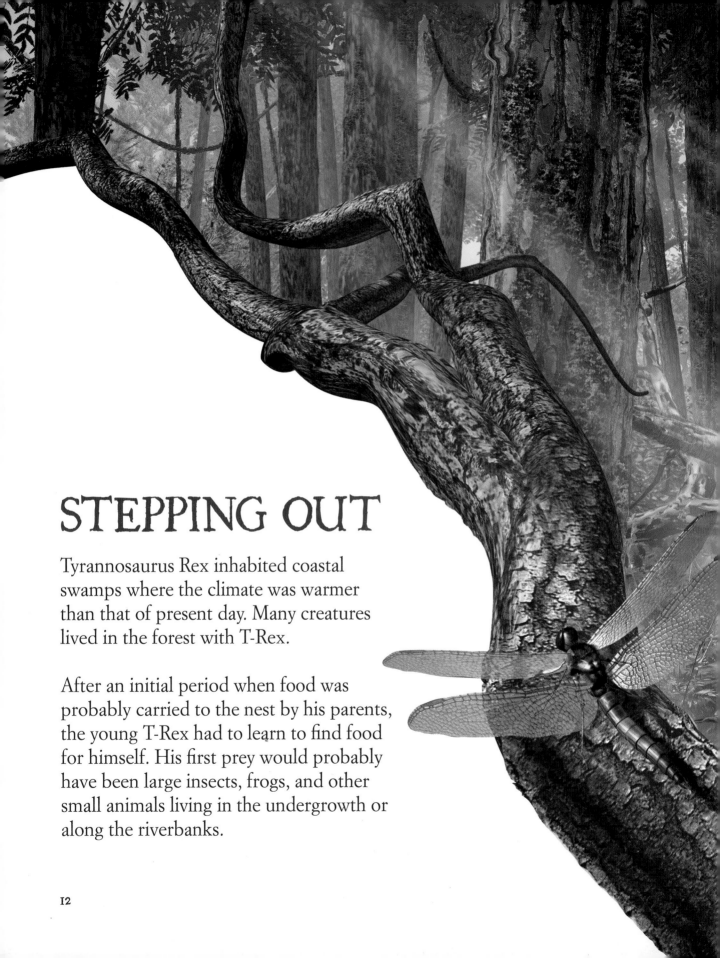

STEPPING OUT

Tyrannosaurus Rex inhabited coastal swamps where the climate was warmer than that of present day. Many creatures lived in the forest with T-Rex.

After an initial period when food was probably carried to the nest by his parents, the young T-Rex had to learn to find food for himself. His first prey would probably have been large insects, frogs, and other small animals living in the undergrowth or along the riverbanks.

LIFE LESSONS

Tyrannosaurus Rex was the largest predator of its time. Although its large body did not allow T-Rex to run at high speeds, it could hunt plant-eating dinosaurs by ambush.

Hidden in the vegetation, the T-Rex waited for passing prey and leaped out suddenly, catching them. Luckily for T-Rex, its preferred prey, the duckbilled Edmontosaurus and the bulky Triceratops, were not skillful runners.

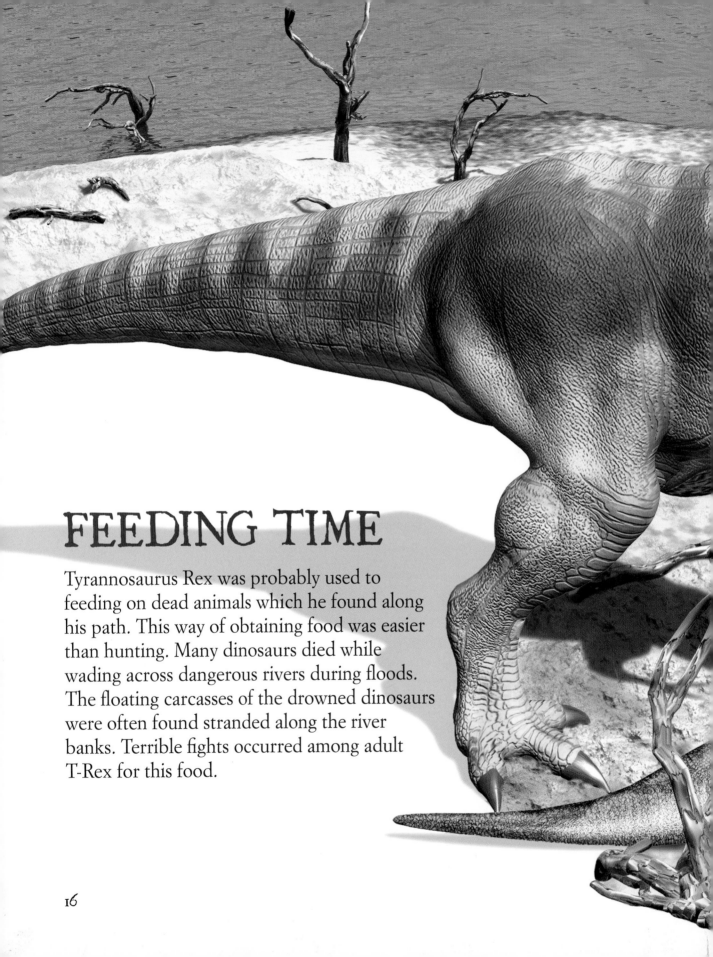

FEEDING TIME

Tyrannosaurus Rex was probably used to feeding on dead animals which he found along his path. This way of obtaining food was easier than hunting. Many dinosaurs died while wading across dangerous rivers during floods. The floating carcasses of the drowned dinosaurs were often found stranded along the river banks. Terrible fights occurred among adult T-Rex for this food.

INSIDE T-REX

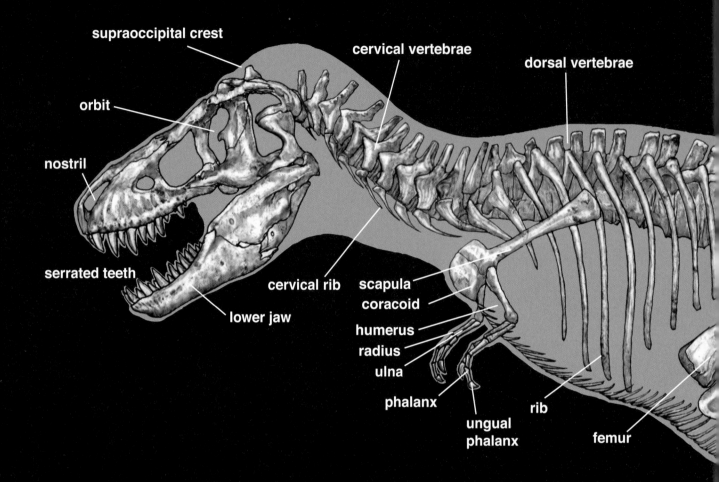

supraoccipital crest

cervical vertebrae

dorsal vertebrae

orbit

nostril

serrated teeth

lower jaw

cervical rib

scapula

coracoid

humerus

radius

ulna

phalanx

ungual phalanx

rib

femur

The Tyrannosaur skeleton had a large skull supported by a short neck and a long tail. The powerful hind limb ended with a strong foot with three toes with pointed claws and a fourth toe facing backward. The front limbs of T-Rex were small and had only two fingers.

When moving, T-Rex kept his body horizontal and in line with his tail, which did not touch the ground. T-Rex were bipeds, which means they walked on their hind limbs alone, balancing the weight of their big head with their large tail. Some scholars believe the T-Rex could run 45 miles per hour (72 km/h), but 12.5 to 25 miles an hour (20–40 km/h) is more likely.

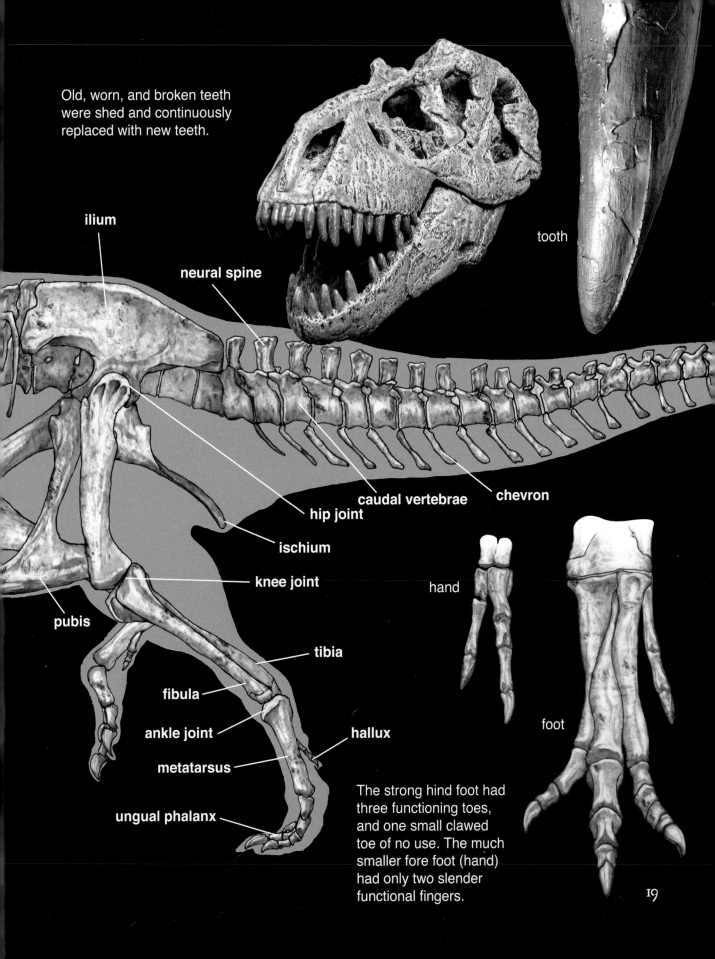

Old, worn, and broken teeth were shed and continuously replaced with new teeth.

tooth

ilium

neural spine

caudal vertebrae

chevron

hip joint

ischium

knee joint

hand

pubis

tibia

fibula

ankle joint

hallux

metatarsus

foot

ungual phalanx

The strong hind foot had three functioning toes, and one small clawed toe of no use. The much smaller fore foot (hand) had only two slender functional fingers.

19

FINDING T-REX FOSSILS

In 1902, the first skeleton of a Tyrannosaurus Rex was discovered in Montana, by the paleontologist Barnum Brown. In 1905, Henry F. Osborn named the fossil Tyrannosaurus ("tyranta lizard") Rex ("king") because of its enormous size.

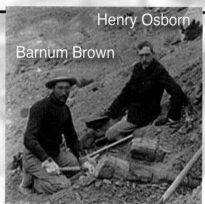
Henry Osborn
Barnum Brown

Tyrannosaurus Rex fossils are found in rocks from ancient rivers and lakes. Sometimes the large dinosaurs died near the rivers because of disease or accidents. During floods the water carried the T-Rex bodies away and deposited them on the bottom of the river. During the transport the bodies were broken apart, so full fossil skeletons of large dinosaurs like T-Rex are rare.

The most recent and sensational discovery has been that of Sue (it is a custom among dinosaur hunters to give a nickname to the mostly complete skeletons). Sue is a nearly complete skeleton of a large Tyrannosaurus, with 85-90% of the original bones preserved. Sue is now on exhibit at the Field Museum of Chicago.

Other important T-Rex skeletons are exhibited at the American Museum of Natural History, New York City, and at The Carnegie Museum, Pittsburgh, where they tower above visitors in the dinosaur rooms.

A juvenile specimen, with the nickname "Tinker," is at the Museum of Natural History in Cleveland, Ohio.

New skeletons are continuously discovered and other museums are added to the list of those exhibiting a T-Rex.

- Spinosaurus, Northern Africa, 95–100 million years ago

- Carcharodontosaurus, Northern Africa, 95–100 million years ago

- Allosaurus, United States, 148–155 million years ago

- Giganotosaurus, Argentina, 93–110 million years ago

22

THE BIGGEST THEROPODS

Discovery sites of the
largest carnivorous dinosaurs
shown on these pages.

Tyrannosaurus,
United States and Canada,
65 million years ago

THE GREAT EXTINCTION

Tyrannosaurus Rex was one of the last dinosaurs. Sixty-five million years ago, dinosaurs became extinct. Scientists think a large meteorite hitting the earth caused this extinction. A wide crater caused by a meteorite exactly 65 million years ago has been located along the coast of Mexico. The dust suspended in the air by the impact would have obscured the sunlight for a long time, causing a drastic drop in temperature and killing many plants.

The plant-eating dinosaurs would have starved or frozen to death. T-Rex and other meat-eating dinosaurs would have also died without their food supply. However, some scientists believe dinosaurs did not die out completely, and that present-day chickens and other birds are, in a way, the descendants of the large dinosaurs.

A DINOSAUR'S FAMILY TREE

The oldest dinosaur fossils are 220–225 million years old and have been found all over the world.

Dinosaurs are divided into two groups. Saurischians are similar to reptiles, with the pubic bone directed forward, while the Ornithischians are like birds, with the pubic bone directed backward.

Saurischians are subdivided in two main groups: Sauropodomorphs, to which quadrupeds and vegetarians belong; and Theropods, which include bipeds and predators.

Ornithischians are subdivided into three large groups: Thyreophorans which include the quadrupeds Stegosaurians and Ankylosaurians; Ornithopods; and Marginocephalians subdivided into the bipedal Pachycephalosaurians and the mainly quadrupedal Ceratopsians.

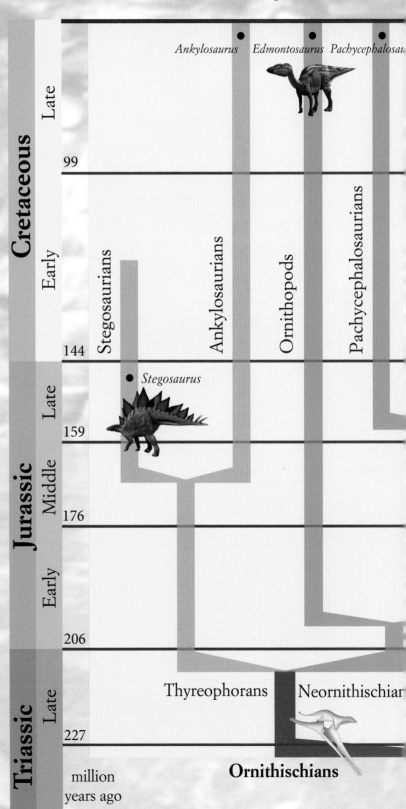

Ankylosaurus   Edmontosaurus   Pachycephalosau

Stegosaurus

Stegosaurians
Ankylosaurians
Ornithopods
Pachycephalosaurians

Thyreophorans   Neornithischiar

Ornithischians

Period		Epoch	million years ago
Cretaceous		Late	
			99
		Early	
			144
Jurassic		Late	
			159
		Middle	
			176
		Early	
			206
Triassic		Late	
			227

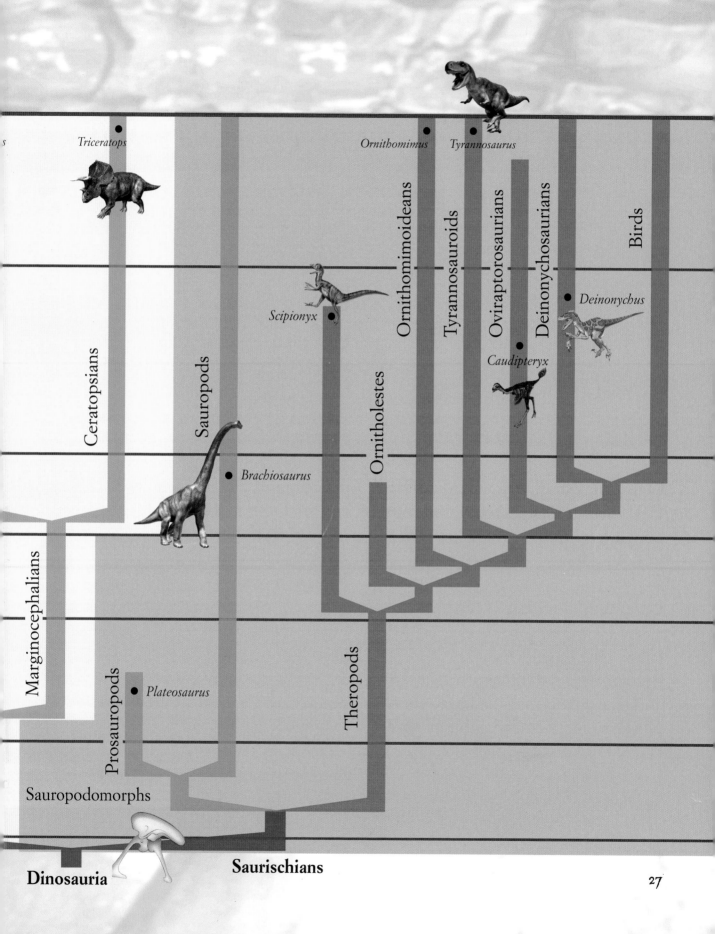

Triceratops

Ornithomimus

Tyrannosaurus

Ornithomimoideans

Tyrannosauroids

Oviraptorosaurians

Deinonychosaurians

Deinonychus

Birds

Ceratopsians

Scipionyx

Caudipteryx

Sauropods

Ornitholestes

Brachiosaurus

Marginocephalians

Theropods

Prosauropods

Plateosaurus

Sauropodomorphs

Dinosauria

Saurischians

A SHORT VOCABULARY OF DINOSAURS

Bipedal: pertaining to an animal moving on two feet alone, almost always those of the hind legs.

Bone: hard tissue made mainly of calcium phosphate; single element of the skeleton.

Carnivore: a meat-eating animal.

Caudal: pertaining to the tail.

Cenozoic Era (Caenozoic, Tertiary Era): the interval of geological time between 65 million years ago and present day.

Cervical: pertaining to the neck.

Claws: the fingers and toes of predator animals end with pointed and sharp nails, called claws. Those of plant-eaters end with blunt nails, called hooves.

Cretaceous Period: the interval of geological time between 144 and 65 million years ago.

Egg: a large cell enclosed in a porous shell produced by reptiles and birds to reproduce themselves.

Epoch: a division of geologic time.

Evolution: changes in the character states of organisms, species and higher ranks through time.

Feathers: outgrowth of the skin of birds and some other dinosaurs, used in flight and in providing insulation and protection of the body. They evolved from reptilian scales.

Forage: to wander in search of food.

Fossil: evidence of the life in the past. Not only bones, but footprints and trails made by animals, as well as dung, eggs, or plant resin, when fossilized, is a fossil.

Herbivore: a plant-eating animal.

Jurassic Period: the interval of geological time between 206 and 144 million years ago.

Mesozoic Era (Mesozoic, Secondary Era): the interval of the geological time between 248 and 65 million years ago.

Pack: a group of predator animals acting together to capture the prey.

Paleontologist: scientists who study and reconstruct prehistoric life.

Paleozoic Era (Paleozoic, Primary Era): the interval of geological time between 570 and 248 million years ago.

Predator: an animal that preys on other animals for food.

Raptor (raptorial): a bird of prey, such as an eagle, hawk, falcon, or owl.

Rectrix (plural rectrices): any of the larger feathers in a bird's tail that are important in helping its flight direction.

Scavenger: an animal that eats dead animals.

Skeleton: a structure of animal body made of several different bones. One primary function is also to protect delicate organs such as the brain, lungs, and heart.

Skin: the external, thin layer of the animal body. Skin cannot fossilize unless it is covered by scales, feathers, or fur.

Skull: bones that protect the brain and the face.

Teeth: tough structures in the jaws used to hold, cut, and sometimes process food.

Terrestrial: living on land.

Triassic Period: the interval of geological time between 248 and 206 million years ago.

Vertebrae: the single bones of the backbone; they protect the spinal cord.

DINOSAUR WEBSITES

Dinosaur Train (pbskids.com/dinosaurtrain/): From the PBS show Dinosaur Train, you can have fun watching videos, printing out pages to color, play games, and learn lots of facts about so many dinosaurs!

The Natural History Museum (http://www.nhm.ac.uk/kids-only/dinosaurs/): Take a quiz to see how much you know about dinosaurs or a quiz to tell you what type of dinosaur you'd be! There's also a fun directory of dinosaurs, including some cool 3D views of your favorites.

Discovery Channel Dinosaur videos (http://dsc.discovery.com/video-topics/other/dinosaur-videos): Watch almost 100 videos about the life of dinosaurs!

Dinosaurs for Kids (www.kidsdinos.com): There's basic information about most dinosaur types, and you can play dinosaur games, vote for your favorite dinosaur, and learn about the study of dinosaurs, paleontology.

MUSEUMS

Yale Peabody Museum of Natural History, 170 Whitney Avenue, New Haven, CT 06520-8118

American Museum Natural History, Central Park West at 79th Street, New York, NY 10024-5192

The Field Museum, 1400 So. Lake Shore Drive, Chicago, IL 60605-2496

Carnegie Museum of Natural History, 4400 Forbes Avenue, Pittsburgh, PA 15213-4080

National Museum of Natural History, the Smithsonian Institution, 10th Street and Constitution Avenue NW, Washington, DC 20560-0136

Museum of the Rockies, 600 W. Kagy Boulevard, Bozeman, MT 59717

Denver Museum of Nature and Science, 2001 Colorado Boulevard, Denver, CO 80205

Dinosaur National Monument, Highway 40, Dinosaur, CO 81610

Sam Noble Museum of Natural History, 2401 Chautauqua, Norman, OK 73072-7029

Museum of Paleontology, University of California, 1101 Valley Life Sciences Bldg, Berkeley, CA 94720-4780

Royal Tyrrell Museum of Palaeontology, Hwy 838, Drumheller, AB T0J 0Y0, Canada

INDEX

Page numbers in **boldface** are images.
· ·